Loving You

by

Brynne Aidlin-Perlman

Cover art by Eyal Pery

For all of the people
who are in these words.
To the ones who know it,
and the ones who don't.

Sections:

Introduction

1. Unrequited Love

2. Hope

3. Life

4. Love

5. Heartbreak

6. Depression

7. Moving On

Introduction

Beginnings are always the most difficult part of a story. That is what this is, after all. A story. My book holds my emotions, my experiences, what I have learned, how I view the world, and how I have changed.

I write to heal and explain myself and to touch the lives of other people. Sometimes I write exactly what I feel. Sometimes I write about what I have felt in the past. Sometimes I look out the window of a car or walk through a mall and am randomly inspired by an idea that pops into my head. Maybe the poem doesn't turn out the way I had planned, but I've learned in life that little ever does. And sometimes the world is more beautiful for it.

The writing in these pages is inspired from the poetry on my Instagram account, @L0ving.you, the inspiration for the title of this book. I chose the order of this story carefully. Each poem tells its own story, the writing within a section tells a story, and the book as a whole tells a story. It was amazing to discover how two pieces written a year apart, about completely different situations, from completely different places in my life, could be so cohesive.

After choosing the pieces and sections I wanted and deciding the order of them, I discovered what my book was really about: ever after. Throughout these pages, I mention that idea again and again. Maybe it isn't always a happily ever after, and it most certainly isn't the ever after I expected, but it exists. Because just as stories begin, stories also end. In a beautifully unexpected way.

When I sat down to write this story, I was filled with excitement by the idea of people holding my words in their hands. Not only people I have never met, but people I see every day. Maybe they are able to more deeply understand me. Maybe someone in these words picks up this book, without knowing they exist here. Maybe even after they read the book, they won't know that some of the words are for them, which is why this book is dedicated to everyone I wrote about, whether they know it or not.

I hope this book helps you. Whether it is the entire book, or just one section, or just one poem. If I can impact someone, I have told my story in a way that helps others complete their own. I have helped others find their ever after.

The ever after I found for myself in creating this book has opened a door for me to start a new story. That beginning will take me to my next ever after. Any moment can be the closing of a chapter. Any moment can be the opening of a book with new words and new memories. Life is constantly opening books and giving me opportunities. And I am experiencing life in the most passionate way I know how.

Unrequited Love

This is how the story starts. You fall in love with someone who does not love you back. You experience the pain of not being wanted, the heartache of rejection, the suffering of pining away for someone who just isn't interested.

Like I said, beginnings are never easy. But taking the first step with this section is the only way to start since my story began with a boy who did not care about me. Throughout my life, I have loved unreachable people, and I know that unrequited love can be ugly and painful, but I take that pain and create beauty. The whole reason I started writing poetry was because of that pain, after all. Sometimes the best results come from the worst situations, just like unrequited love itself. Although it hurts us, it teaches us and helps us grow.

Through the fantasizing about what could be, the wondering over what was, and the agonizing over what is, always remember you deserve love. There is a happily ever after waiting for you. You are simply still at the beginning, still at the *once upon a time...*

"Fairytale"

once upon a time,
a girl fell in love with a boy
who did not love her back.

"Unwritten"

write me another book, another story,
one with different words and different pages,
one that is happy and joyful, one that you
smile when you read, not one where you cry
and want to throw the book in the fire.

write me another book where the
beginning, middle, and end are happy and
my life works out the way it should.

write me another book where
i have the boy i always dreamed of.

"Gravity"

when the world told me to stop loving you,
my heart kept beating with
your name as the rhythm.
my brain kept wandering to thoughts of you
as if you were fuel for my mind.
my entire body rang with
wanting your touch as my rib cage
dared to let go of the feelings
being kept bottled up.

because the world told me to stop loving you.
but the earth never asked permission
to circle around the sun;
the sun just pulled it right in.

"Held"

i want to flaunt you, show you off.
i want to hold your hand in public.
i want to take pictures of you kissing me.
i want to brag about how amazing you are.
but i cannot do any of this.

instead i whisper that you are mine,
privately,
when no one is around to hear it.

and instead,
we take no pictures together.
not even one.
not even at all.

and instead,
i hold your name between my hands
like the morning sunrise
because you are something beautiful
that i can never truly capture,
never truly
have.

"Deception"

you can't
look at me like that
and expect me to believe
you don't have feelings for me.
because your eyes
they say,
i care.
they say,
i care so much.

but maybe you taught me that
eyes
are beautiful liars.

"Transforming"

i changed myself so you would love me
just to realize you never would.
-    *maybe if i had been myself,*
    you would have loved me back.

"Recollection"

i know you never really knew me.
all you knew was my name and i am sure by now
you have forgotten even that.
you do not ever think about me because
i have vanished from your memory.
i am a ghost you do not recognize.

i try to be okay with that,
but every day the only thought on my mind is you.
and you have no idea what it is like
to love someone who does not even
remember who you are.

"Injustice"

it isn't fair
that people can exist
and i can fall in love
and they do not even know
who i am.

"Faucet"

it
hurts so much that
i am never going to be able to
show him all of myself.
he is never going to know
the poetry that speaks to me.
he is never going to know
the songs i love or
the books that touch my heart.
he is never going to know
how much he meant to me.
he is never going to know.
because i am going on with my life
and he is going on with his,
and he will never know
that i loved him with
every broken piece of my heart.

"Unanswered Questions"

why does he not give me time?
why does he not care?
why does he pretend to care when he doesn't?
why does he say maybe when
the answer is always no?
why does he lie?
why does he hurt me?
why do i think about him constantly when he
doesn't think about me at all?

why do i write poems and dedicate
pages to someone who will never know
they are for him?
why will he not miss me when i am gone?
why am i too afraid to ask him any of this?
why do i still love him after all of it?

why?

"Disappointment"

gripping onto you and
trying not to let go,
but i knew that eventually
you would choose her.

maybe in another time,
later on in our lives,
when you realize i loved you,
everything will turn out fine and
reality will fall away
like a blindfold.

but you do not choose me
and reality is a slap in the face
because you do not love me
or even think about me.
your love belongs to her.

"Sufficiency"

there has to be a way to explain
the pain i feel
when i watch you
kiss her.
because the words
heartbreak
sadness
jealousy
wanting
longing
do not do it
justice.

"Universe"

you are my sun,
but i am just another star in your galaxy.

"Ninety-Three Million Miles"

can't you see it?
how happy you make her,
how much she smiles when you are around?
can't you see it?
in the way she looks at you,
in the way she talks to you?

see it.
because she wants you to see it
without saying a word.
because she wants you to say it first.
she wants you to be happy.
she wants you to smile.
she wants you.
stop putting a blindfold over your eyes
and embrace the fact that she cares.
see her for all she is. tell her if she matters to you.
do not let a chance slip between your fingers.

she is sunlight. she is beautiful.
she is choosing to shine on you.
she shines brightest in your presence.
see the sun. see it.
see her.

"Second Choice"

but you chose someone else.
after all of the sacrifices i made for you,
all of the times i
dropped my life to help you,
all of the times i gave you advice
while you were close to tears.

i gave you so much energy,
so much time. and in the end,
you chose the person who hurt you.
you chose the person who caused you pain,
the person who broke your heart.
the person whose mess
i helped clean up.

(i guess i didn't matter all that much.)

"Command"

i think you would laugh
if you knew how much of my writing
is about you.
- *you told me to keep writing,*
  but did you know
  all i write about is you?

"Pouring"

how can giving you everything
mean absolutely nothing?

"Acceptance"

i accepted it really and truly.
i felt it shift in my heart, i felt it deep in my bones.
it was a calm kind of realization,
as if peace was washing over me slowly.

but how can peace leave me aching?
how can peace leave me empty?
my heart hurts with the weight of the truth
because even though i accepted it,
for that split second it hurt like hell.
as i watched him talk about her,
the way his eyes lit up,
i saw on his face how much he loves her.

and i knew that already.
but when i heard it from his mouth,
the mouth i have dreamed of kissing,
it made it real and true.

and there is no emotion more bitter than
accepting excruciating truth, no feeling sweeter
than that calm and peace,
no heartbreak more bittersweet than knowing
the person you love is happy
and knowing they do not love you.

"Expectations"

this is my apology to you.
my way to say sorry for what i caused.
my apology for
expecting love from you
that i could never have.
my apology for my heart breaking
over the thought of us
that was impossible to reach.

i am sorry.
i am sorry i loved you when i should have known
you would never love me.

"Ache"

your words are empty.
filled with so much
but none of it
for me.

"Where It Started"

it all started with you.
i loved you more than i have ever loved anyone,
but you broke my heart so badly that
two years later i am still picking up the pieces.
i did move on from you.
i do not love you anymore.
i hardly ever think about you.

but it did start with you.
ever since i fell in love with you,
everyone i fall for seems to love someone else.
it is like you started a chain of people
who i would love and would never love me.
it is like you started a curse.
you started endless and ongoing pain in my life.
i know that logically
it cannot be blamed on you, but
i still find myself connecting it back.

"Questions That Won't Fade"

what if he didn't mean to hurt me?
what if i misunderstood his actions and words?
maybe it was my fault all along and
i needed to give him more time.
maybe he did love me.

then again,
i already let him go so it is easier to think
he knew that what he was doing was breaking me
than to believe
i actually had a chance.

"Transparency"

I once fell in love with a boy
who I thought loved me back.
But as time passed, I
realized what he lacked.
He lacked the ability to say that
his heart belonged to someone else.
So he left me there alone, all by myself.
I had to figure out that he wasn't the one.
And I promise you this: it was the
hardest thing I've ever done.

"Two-Faced"

maybe he does know how you feel.
maybe he knows and, whether consciously or not,
he takes satisfaction in that.
he is happy that someone cares about him,
and that is why he gives you those mixed signals.
even though he doesn't like you,
part of him likes the idea of it.
that is why you think
the moments you share are so special:
you see the part of him that
likes the game you play.

but sometimes he reveals the side of him
that does not care at all.
maybe that is why you cannot give up on him,
you think you have a chance.
but why do you still love him when
it is clear
he does not love you?

"What You Deserve"

give up on him.
not because you are over him,
but because at a certain point
you need to learn that you are
worth being loved back.

<u>Hope</u>

Hope builds up our lives, surrounding us in every moment. We cling to hope like it is our lifeline, like it keeps us afloat. We always want to believe in the happily ever after we know we deserve. Hope is like a rubber band: it constantly pulls harsh reality farther and farther away, but eventually it will snap back and leave a mark on our skin.

I frequently turn to hope because I believe that situations happen for a reason, and I trust that they happen for an important reason even if I cannot see it in the moment. Sometimes hope acts like a shield from what I do not want to see, but I will never stop relying on an emotion that brings the best out of the worst situations. It offers my heart a chance to see beauty in impossibilities that may or may not come true. It offers my heart a chance to see an ever after, even if that ever after cannot be reached. When I want to stop hoping, when I want to let go of believing, life always has a way of bringing hope back to my doorstep. I will always be grateful for that.

Have hope. Always believe. Do not forget about the bad, but do not release the good. Do not let go of hope. Do not let go of your lifeline.

"Farsighted"

it is a wild creature, my heart.
it breaks and throws itself back into battle.
it doesn't think.
it doesn't remember pain.
it only believes that it could end well this time
because hope has poisoned my heart
and hope only cares about
the what could be,
the if,
the maybe,
not the truth.
it is blind to what is in its line of sight
and chooses to focus on the horizon
which holds infinite what could be,
if, and maybe.

and that wild creature called my heart,
poisoned by the idea of hope,
only sees the horizon,
only sees the possibilities,
only sees that
dreams are so much better than
cold harsh reality.

"Return"

my hope has been shattered
so many times.
every heartbreak, every time someone
didn't like me back, yet

i.
still.
hope.

and my brain screams at me to stop hoping
on impossibilities,
on daydreams,
on situations i should never hope for.
but my heart is wild and it
won't stop hoping.

"Realization"

he is never going to know all of me.
i wrote it.
the truth.
it is there.
in front of my eyes.

and yet,
i look the other direction.
and yet,
i push it away as hard as i can.
and yet,
i ignore it as long as i can.

because i love him
and i want him to know all of me.

"Ember"

i hang onto his words and actions and our
small, seemingly stupid moments
as if they are a lifeline.
because they are all i have.
they are all i can ever have.
words exchanged, jokes created, smiles shared,
memories flickering and fading away
faster than a
single ember on wet wood.

i know i should stop
feeding a fire that cannot start,
should stop putting so much
energy and thought to an impossible task.
yet that single ember is better than any fire.
i will not stop hoping that
my ember will become a fire
though i shouldn't,
though it can't.

but the hope of what that ember could
potentially become is too great to pass up,
to let go of, to just
give away.

"Windows to the Soul"

i know you don't love me,
i'm not stupid.
but when you look at me like that,
how can you expect me not to have
a little bit of *hope?*

"Standing Up"

choose your battles wisely.
sometimes you do not need to fight because
it just isn't worth it.
they say not to fight battles
you know you cannot win,
but sometimes those are the battles
that are most worth fighting.

"Small Hands"

some people grab onto everything
or they at least try to.
but *everything* slips between your fingers
like love
because *everything* cannot be
held or felt or touched.
because as soon as *everything* is in your hand
there is something new,
and grabbing onto that something new
means letting go of something old.

so truly,
everything is not a realistic thought.
it is simply a dream to spark hope
in an idea that can never be reached.

"Gallery"

i am someone who feels strongly that
people need to know who i am,
need to know the real me.
i want people to talk to me and know
what happens in my head.
i pour out my emotions and
leave them on display like they are
part of a museum.

i don't know why i do that.
i don't know why i reveal what is
going on in my mind
to people who do not care.
i don't know why i tell them everything
when it will change nothing.
i hope one day i will accept that
not everyone i come across will know
every opinion i have or learn every lesson
i have learned.
but right now i want everyone to
see me the way i see myself.
i am hoping on an impossibility,
and that is the problem.

"Out of Reach"

i feel like i am carrying memories i do not have, moments that have not happened to me, all of the situations that go on in my head, the conversations and events that my brain comes up with. even though i have not actually experienced it, it feels like every day i drag it along, like every day it burdens me. my mind comes up with these elaborate stories with people where i grow close to them and it is like i expect to see them and it will all be different, as if they actually did what they did in my head, as if what happened in my brain also happened in reality.

i know they will not know about any of it, but that is when i feel isolated. when i am looking at that person i lived through an entire story with the night before and the world keeps spinning the same way it did as if what happened in my head didn't matter.

it hurts to have so much baggage from thousands of universes i have created and never be able to see the impact it made because it never left any impact at all. it is just another reminder that i hang on and others don't, that i remember and others forget. it is so much to carry around and it feels like i am trapped under an avalanche, searching and searching for oxygen that cannot reach me.

"Paradox"

i hate creating moments
that cannot happen.
hate imagining conversations
that are impossible,
hate building beliefs made of paper thin hope,
hate loving unreachable people only to be
loved by those who i did not ask to love me.

i hate loving because loving means hoping
and hoping means losing and
losing means breaking my heart over
someone i should not have
loved in the first place.
i hate that i am the kind of girl
who lives in my own head and lets my
heart grow attached to what i create.
but i hate that i do not hate it at all.
i hate that those parts of me form who i am.
i hate that i love it even when it hurts me.

love and hate. hate and love.
tied together with a knot.
and i cannot untie them to figure out if
maybe i hate what i love or if maybe
i love what i hate and
maybe it is both
and maybe i am a paradox
that cannot ever be explained.

"Process of Elimination"

i have always known that
i care too much.
i have always known the pain
of people not thinking about me as much as i
think about them,
but i never tied it together.
or maybe i knew there was a knot
without knowing how it became tied.
and i see it so clearly now
i feel ridiculous for not realizing it sooner.

i think about life so much,
the moments
the people,
because i want them to care as much as i do,
and i care more.
if i do not think about it
i know they aren't either,
but if i do think about it, i can
hold onto some hope that they are, too.
  -   *i think i explained myself.*

"Foundation"

that is what hope is about, after all.
giving people
a place to stand,
giving people
a handle to grab onto.

"Intermixed"

hope does not follow reason or logic.
hope has no rules.
it will reach out and show you
impossibilities that can never come true.
just like love.

love cannot be bound or tied up.
love cannot be defined.
love cannot be controlled because
love does not follow rules, either.
love will envelope you in
moments you do not expect it.
you will enjoy someone's laugh or smile or eyes
or the way their voice sounds and
all of a sudden love is there,
ready to embrace you.

love can hurt; love can heal.
hope can destroy; hope can mend.
it is about taking the bad and the good
because
you cannot have the latter without the former.

"Limitless"

hope
starts out small and
morphs to be
big and beautiful and consuming.
like a plant
that starts with a seed
and grows into
a tree.
with roots keeping it grounded
and branches reaching for the stars,
branches reaching for everything
that can possibly exist.

"Figurative"

looking for strength.
finding a metaphor for myself.
i might see a kite and imagine i
can also fly among the clouds.
i can be a tree,
or a flower,
or words on a page.
anything.
a*ll*.

Life

Life holds our memories with each other, our love, our happiness, and our pain. It is not always sunny skies and rainbows. There are storms that rip apart what we know, hurricanes that destroy what we love, and tornadoes that steal what we have. But life always has a way to teach us what we need. It becomes our ever after.

I go through the ups and downs of life. Sometimes I enjoy the company of friends and family, or the sound of music in my ears, or the feeling of the ocean against my ankles, and I know exactly why life is a gift. Even through the times where I ache at what those storms take from me, I know that life always has a way to sort out situations. Maybe not the way I expected it or wanted it, but I know that I am learning what I am learning and experiencing what I am experiencing because life is unpredictably wild chaos, like the weather. One day it is sunny, the next I am surrounded in fog. But when the fog clears, I see where I am meant to go.

Live for the moments of beauty despite the hurricanes and tornadoes. We are here to be alive and live every single moment to the fullest.

"Living Is"

living is creating inside jokes with your friends.
living is cooking s'mores around a bonfire
late at night.

living is falling asleep curled up in someone's arms.
is reading a book that makes you cry.
is singing in the shower.
is watching a horror movie.
is laughing until tears stream down your face.
is meeting people who
touch your life profoundly
even if you will never see them again.

living is screaming on a rollercoaster.
is swimming in the ocean.
is taking selfies.
is writing poetry.
is looking at the stars and moon.
is watching the sunset.
living is every moment you are being yourself.
is being with people you love.
is loving.

living is hearing your heartbeat and
knowing you love the sound.
it is knowing you are here to travel the world
and experience hope and pain and
heartache and happiness.

living is all around me.
i am alive.
i am alive every second of my life.

"Destination"

the choices we make,
the paths that we choose,
do not define
who we are; they lead us
to who we are going to become.

"The Little Things"

the little things.
they pile up like tiny pieces of paper,
like discarded memories, like forgotten moments.
they create
giant looming mountains and empty homes.
they burn like hot embers
in a fireplace.

but sometimes we forget that
too many embers can start a fire.
just like we forget that
the little things,
when put together,
aren't so little
and can come together to burn
bright and hot and destroy
everything they touch.

so always remember that the little things,
those tiny pieces of paper,
those forgotten moments,
those empty homes, those embers,
(those embers)
have power
because the little things are actually
the big things.

"Sunset"

we are here
on this earth
living life for decades and decades.
but
what do we leave behind?

and that is so
terrifying
because sometimes i wonder
if eventually i will just be
forgotten,
non-existent.
if i will just fade away from the picture
like the sun disappears
beyond the
horizon.

"Perseverance"

it feels like i am living life
in the wrong direction,
like i am climbing up a down escalator.
always trying to reach the top,
always trying to achieve my goal,
but falling short every time.

because i keep fighting,
i never give up.
yet life seems to pull me down
without caring about
how hard i
fight.

"Body Image"

my legs
have never been skinny like
the twigs you find on the ground.
my stomach
has never been flat like
the ocean on a calm day.
my body
has never been perfect like
the girls in the magazines, and
society has tried to make me feel guilty
for that.

but why should i?
why should i feel guilty for taking up space?
why should i feel guilty for
my legs
that stand tall like tree trunks,
supporting me wherever i stand?

why should i feel embarrassed for
my stomach
that carries life in its waves and
does not apologize for being wild?

why should i feel remorse for
my body
that may not be enough for society
but is enough
for me.

"Unique"

he called me "special."
just like that.
with quotes around the word.
as if it was an insult,
as if he meant to hurt me.

but i would rather be "special"
than boring.
and i would rather be "special"
than be like everyone else.
and maybe in his mind
"special" is a dagger because
the quotes are a way for him to cover the fact
that i am just special.
without the quotes, without the insult,
without the hurt or pain.

i am special.
and that is too much for him to understand
because he is afraid of what
special
actually means.

"Your Power"

those things.
those things called words.
they are beautiful.
they can be molded together to
build entire stories,
entire worlds.

but those things,
those things called words.
that are so beautiful,
that can build entire stories and worlds,
can tear apart love.
so be careful when you decide to use
those things called words.

"Full Circle"

perhaps you learn how to
treat others
based on the way you
treat yourself.

perhaps you learn how to
treat yourself
based on the way
others treat you.

"Conformity"

people always make assumptions.
i just feel i either
confine myself to those assumptions
despite them being wrong
or feel strongly i have to
defy those assumptions even if
they are correct.

and sometimes i do not know which
i am doing or if i am actually
thinking and feeling for myself.

"What Really Matters"

at the end of the day,
age is irrelevant.
it is about our wisdom, our dedication,
our willingness to be kind.
it is about our ability to
spread laughter and our strength to
rise after we fall.
it is about what we have learned and
how we apply it to our lives.
it is about what we cope with
and how we let it change us.

age is just a number we use to measure
how long we have been alive.
it measures our years,
not our understanding of the world.
life is about what we have experienced
and what we learn from it.

some people close themselves off from others
because of a number that means so little.

"The Irony"

the people who are the best at understanding
are the worst at being understood.

"Timezone"

they say
even a broken clock is right twice a day,
and it is true.
when the clock stops working,
when the clock pauses and is stuck in the past,
when it cannot move its hands and
keep ticking forward,
eventually time will catch up and
it will be right.

but what about a clock that just
says the wrong time
and keeps ticking despite it?
what about a clock that is not stuck
but continues to move
despite being broken,
despite being incorrect,
never finding its way back to where it should be,
never finding its way out of the timezone
it is trapped in?

"Flimsy"

time.
such a silly word,
an idea made of paper.
a word we invented,
a concept that doesn't really exist.
and yet,
we are all obsessed with it.
we cannot get enough.

why?
why are we so hooked on a thought
that can evaporate?
why do we care so much about a feeling
that confines us?
why do we bother wasting our breath
on a word
that doesn't even
matter?

"Present"

why was i living life in the future?
why was i waiting to start living life in
five, ten, fifteen years?
life is now.
life is all around me.
life isn't in
five
ten
fifteen years.
it is now.
in my family, in my friends, in my writing,
in every day.

the future is never promised.
tomorrow is not promised.
ten years from now is not promised.
but now is promised.
this moment is promised.
do not live for moments that
have not happened yet.
live
for now.

"Second Chances"

i always complain that
if i were able to
live my life again,
i would change so much,
but eventually i realized
i would have lived the
exact same way.
every choice i made,
every mistake i regretted,
built me into who i am and
brought me to where i am now.

i would not trade that for anything.

"Gift"

i will repeat it.
like a melody you cannot release from your head,
like a thought that wiggles its way
passed barriers and throbs against your temples
until you accept it as truth.
like the sun continues to sink and rise back up,
like a waterfall cascades over cliff sides.
like a stone plummets down into
the depths of the sea.

i will repeat it.
like summer arrives with open arms.
like fall drapes a jacket around your shoulders.
like winter enters with a wicked cackle.
like spring blooms flowers in the
darkest crevices of your heart.

i will repeat it.
the same way the world repeats patterns,
the same way life continues on.
and i will repeat it.
i will repeat it over and over.
this world holds promise.
this world holds hope.
this world holds all.
this world is beautiful.

Love

Love is the reason for every action and every moment. Sometimes love sneaks up on us, catches us unaware, bites into our skin with sharp teeth. Sometimes love embraces and fixes us. Love shows us the beauty in people and places and moments and memories. Love shows us the beauty within ourselves.

I know love when it looks me in the face and says hello. And love knows me. Every time love breaks me, every time I fall for someone and it doesn't work out the way I want, I am collecting memories in order to become the person I am meant to be. I embrace every person and moment and decorate them with love. Even when love leaves me, love always returns somewhere I never expect to find it. Love is how I know the air in my lungs has purpose, the life I live is filled with meaning, and that everywhere I go, there are pieces of my heart.

Keep loving. Keep giving. Because love will hurt you and love will leave you, but love will also look you in the eyes, take your hand, and remind you exactly why you held on.

"Elements"

your touch is fire.
it warms even the coldest places inside of me.
i curl up beside the fire because
that is where i feel safe.

your voice is water,
running water.
dripping slowly but steadily,
comforting me.

your laugh is air.
gentle
like bells.
enveloping me from all directions.

your gaze is earth,
grounding me.
keeping my feet planted because
you are my gravity.

you.
you are
fire.
water.
air.
earth.
you are all.
everything.

"Habits"

when i close my eyes,
all i see is your charming smile,
beautiful eyes, and adorable laugh.
because the oldest habits are the
easiest to fall back into.
and one of my oldest habits
is falling for you.

no matter what i try to do,
i am always going to come
right back to you.

"All"

He is my sunshine,
he is my rain.
He is my happiness,
he is my pain.
He is my life,
he is my death.
He is my soul,
he is my breath.

He is my *everything*.

"Sweet Tooth"

his eyes were
pools of chocolate
and i was hungry for more.

"Parallel"

despite the fact you are not by my side,
you are going through your day as i am
going through mine.
your heart is beating while my heart is beating.
you are breathing while
i am breathing.

maybe we are both walking or reading or laughing
at the same moment.
we are alive at the same time,
making memories and enjoying every day.
even though we may not physically be together,
we are together in the universe.

"Stay"

i love you,
i love you,
i love you.

maybe if i write it enough times
it will make our chapter
last a little
longer.

"Desperation"

it is all about to fade away.
i am about to fade away.
don't forget me, don't forget me,
please don't forget me.
i need you to hang onto me.
i need you to remember me.

remember me when you forget
what it is like to
lie beside me.
remember me when you forget
the taste of my lips.
remember me
when you forget our first date.
remember me when
you forget my favorite place.

please remember me.
remember my love,
remember my laugh.
remember the details of my face
even when you forget the rest.

"Tragic Transformation"

the worst kind of change is
going from loving someone to losing them.
i used to see you every day,
talk to you every day,
laugh with you every day,
and now i never see you for even one minute.
you are always out of my reach
because our paths were meant to cross and separate,
because we were never meant to stay.

someone told me what you said about me.
i cried.
because i am not there and you still think about me.
because i am not there and you still talk about me.
because you are not here and i still
write poetry about you.
because you are not here and
i still compare everyone i meet to you.
because we are not together but the love still exists.
because we are not together and it hurts.
because we are not together
but we want to be with all of our hearts.

and it is a cruel kind of transformation to go from
loving someone you can hold in your arms to
loving someone you cannot even see.

"You are the Poem"

you are. language.
the letters in words. because
you are my foundation.
the words in sentences. because
you make up everything.
a semicolon. because
you remind me that anything can continue.
a capital letter. because
everything starts with something big.
a comma. because
you know everything connects.
an exclamation point. because
you are excitement.
a question mark. because
you are a mystery.
a period. because
sometimes things just end.
and you don't know why.

"Beg"

you draw the words
please don't go
from my lips
like a confession,
like a secret,
like a part of me is falling from
my mouth
straight into your hands.

"Surprises"

we all lose sight of our feelings.
they run away from us and come back with
realizations that slap us hard across the face.
other times they come from
deep down in a hidden corner
with dark fingers that grab us and pull us under,
so subtly we do not even know what has
come over us.

we do not choose who we fall for.
and falling is terrifying, but it is also exhilarating.
we are caught unaware by someone's
laugh
or smile
or voice
and all of a sudden we are falling and
cannot catch ourselves.

"Former Love"

i may be in love with him now,
but that doesn't mean i don't fall asleep
to the thought of your voice.
i may be in love with him now,
but that doesn't mean i don't still think of you.
i may be in love with him now,
but that doesn't mean i don't wish for
you next to me instead.
i may be in love with him now,
but that doesn't mean i forgot the taste of your lips.
i may be in love with him now, but
that doesn't mean
i am not still in love with you.

"Conflict"

my heart is
screaming your name
while my mind is
whispering his.
    ~   *i don't know which to listen to.*

"Opposition"

you go through life learning opposites.
up and down, left and right,
mean and kind, love and hate.
but the abstract ideas are not so opposite.
there is a fraction between
good and bad treatment,
only an inch between
being kind and being unkind.

sometimes the distance is so small
we confuse them.
sometimes love and hate do not live on
different continents.
sometimes they live right next door with walls
so frail they break as soon as you question them,
letting in a realization you tried to ignore.

sometimes ideas are only opposite because
it is too terrifying to admit we can confuse ourselves
by hanging onto a feeling
that isn't what we are feeling at all.

"Perspective"

love is blind.
love will make you see the good
when there is no good to see.
love will morph your reality
so you no longer know
what is real.

love is blind.
love will hold you close at 11pm
but tear you apart at 3:30am.
love will create mountains when there
isn't even a hill.

love is blind.
love will build entire sculptures when
you only expected a drawing.
love will do whatever it takes to make you believe.
so when they say

love is blind

and you cannot understand why,
it is probably because
love has blinded
you.

"Hands"

but i am lucky, to have these hands.
these hands that
can grab onto so much.
these hands that are worn with
blisters and burns and scars,
these hands that
have carried heavy weights and
dragged me through mud.
these hands that
reach for the light and
try to gain control.

these hands that have touched your hands
have touched your hands
and
these hands that
have held your hands
have held onto you.

"Gratitude"

you
loved me
so fully that
i will always be
complete.

"Open Door"

love is waiting for you.
beyond this pain,
beyond this heartbreak,
beyond the walls you have built for yourself.
it is there.
i promise.
all you have to do is
reach out and
let it in.

"My Relationship with Love"

she smiles and reaches out her hand. i hesitate, unsure
whether to trust her this time, unsure whether she will
leave again. her eyes are bright and hopeful, telling me i
can hang on, telling me she is here now.

but her eyes also say she might leave again. she knows i am
no stranger to that possibility. she has left so often i should
be used to it, but every time it still makes my heart ache.
the question is not how long she will stay, but whether it is
worth it to be with her temporarily, knowing she could
fade away.

i step back from her, and her smile fades, her fingers twitch.
she knows she has hurt me too many times. she knows that
every time she leaves, it knocks the breath from my lungs.
she knows that every time she comes back, i am torn
between falling into her arms or running away from them,
running away from her warm smile, her gentle laugh, her
scattered freckles, her ginger hair.

she knows she has caused me pain, but that is why when
she comes back, she wraps me safely in her arms, caresses
my bruises and heals my scars. she knows me even after all
this time. she still remembers all my corners and edges, still
remembers how to trace my skin and raise goosebumps on
my arms.

and i know her. i know i could never live without her. i
know that every time she returns, the air is put back into
my lungs. i know it is worth it to keep her, even if
temporarily.

i take her hand and she laughs. it is a different laugh now,
a little higher on the ends. it still brings a smile to my lips.
every time she returns, i find home in the familiarity of her

and adoration in the details that have changed. her skin is just as soft as i remember it.

she pulls me into her arms and whispers, "i've missed you." and i tell her all about my new bruises and scars. and i tell love i thought she would never come back. and i tell love i am glad she is here. and i tell love i hope she can stay. and i tell love that even if she can't, i am happy i was able to hold her hand.

Heartbreak

Heartbreak swallows you. You feel the shattered pieces scraping against your throat every time you take a breath. Your heart tries to heal what has been fragmented by people you loved, people you thought would never break you. Through every heartbreak, you continue to trust, to love, and to live.

It is not easy to be betrayed constantly, to keep reconstructing the broken pieces. I have done it time and time again. Sometimes it is only a tiny tap on my glass heart. Sometimes it all crumbles on itself. People are not always careful the way they should be, but I keep giving. I never forget that I have to be cautious, but I also know what I miss if I close myself off, which is why I still give. If I do not share myself with other people, I never have the chance to feel this life dance across my skin and saturate my heart with warmth.

Do not forget the lessons heartbreak teaches you. Do not forget that your heart beats inside your chest with purpose. Do not forget that your heart will rebuild itself. Because your heart was made to survive. Your heart was made to love.

"Event Horizon"

it never kills me.
missing you, wanting you back,
the ache in my heart because you are gone.
it never kills me.

but sometimes i remember the way you smiled,
reaching into your eyes and lighting them up.
the way you looked in the morning,
all messy hair and limbs and the curve of your back
punctuated like an exclamation point.
the way you touched me that made every part of me
sing some sort of wild symphony.
the way you kissed me passionately and fiercely
as if our kiss was what set the sun on fire and
allowed the planets to keep spinning.
the remembering. it never kills me.

but sometimes i remember
how much i loved you, how much you loved me.
and it seems that the light that existed is gone.
and it seems that nothing ends in an
exclamation point because nothing is exciting.
and it seems that there is only silence
because the symphonies have disappeared.
and it seems that the sun has stopped burning,
that the planets have stopped spinning.

it never kills me.
but the pain of missing you
makes me wish it had.

"Leftovers"

but if i was
as pretty as you said,
you would have stayed.
if i mattered
as much as you made it seem,
you would not have walked away.
if you had truly loved me,
you would have
helped me with the broken pieces
you left for me to
clean up.

"Destruction"

you had my heart in your hand and crushed it.
you caused me so much pain that
i cannot even remember the last time i was happy,
and i knew what was best for me, but
i still kept on choosing you.
you should be flattered that i still
love you after i lost myself loving you.
you could destroy every part of me
and obliterate it into ash so that
you might not even remember it was there.
you could absolutely ruin me and
i would let you come back and do it again.

do you know how
heartbreaking that is?
that i love you enough to let you
demolish me as a person?
that i love you more than i love myself?
you will always have the power to ruin me.
and i would let you.
every single time.

"Squinting"

you are the sun.
because you give me life,
because you bring me warmth,
because you supply me with
all i could possibly need.

but sometimes i get so caught up
enjoying your heat and light,
i do not realize what will happen
if i stay too long.
because if you stay too long,
you burn.
your skin turns a bright blistering red and peels away,
leaving you bare and aching and craving to
just one more time
be where the sun shines.

even after everything,
even though i know where i will be if i stay,
i keep letting that light hit me,
i soak it all in.
because i love you enough to let you hurt me.
and even when you leave me burnt,
i will heal and return.
i will always return.

"Out-of-Order"

to him it's a game.
to him you are another girl he can say
he manipulated.
you can get away.
you can stop being mistreated if you just
stop playing the fucking game.

but you can't.
because once you start,
you cannot stop until the
game maker says game over.

"Unwanted"

i am the thought you cannot get rid of,
the one that finds you before you fall asleep.
the one that crawls its way to the
forefront of your mind
in the moments you least expect it.
i inch my way across every bit of your thoughts
until i am there every hour, every minute,
every second.

i know it is painful.
to constantly be reminded of what you left behind,
to always feel the discomfort of the
buzzing in your head.
but how do you think i feel
when thoughts of you crush my brain,
tear their way through my mind,
leaving behind a trail of other thoughts
i will never have because you took their place,
left them bleeding and empty in my littered head?
you ruin everything you touch.
(maybe that is why i am ruined too.)

and insects are an annoyance, an inconvenience.
and i know you wish you could
swat me away, but insects are tolerable;
boulders are not.
remembering what you left is tolerable;
remembering what left you is not.

"Decomposing"

but what do you do when
the person who kept your heart beating leaves?
what do you do when your heart
stops pumping blood to all of your organs,
when your body starts shutting down?

i know that you never actually kept my heart beating,
but it felt like it.
and now you are gone and my flesh is rotting.
i am attracting flies with no will to swat them away.
the scent is burning my nostrils, but
i have no will to fix it because
part of me stupidly hopes that
the smell will find you and you will finally realize
how much you hurt me.

how disgusting.
you ruined me and all i wish for is that
you will notice because i still hope
that you will come back.
and my heart will beat again.
and my heart will pump blood again.
and the flies will disappear.
and the smell of rotting flesh that brought you back
will fade from my memory because
i will have no reason to remember it.

"Natural Disaster"

like a tsunami,
you came crashing into my life.
- *and you left a mess behind.*

"Clarity"

i miss you
and i still love you,
and i would take you back
in a heartbeat.

but you broke me.
and that is something
i can never forgive you for.

"Never Too Late"

do you even understand
the amount of pain you caused me?
do you understand
what you did to me as a person?

you clearly don't.
or i at least hope you don't.
because if you did know, i would like to think
you would have apologized
and you never did.

"Domino Effect"

then it's also my fault, right? for taking it personally
when i know that isn't what he meant?

it is like he hits a domino and walks away and does not
have to deal with the wreckage he leaves behind in my
life since he does not even know it exists. i try to fix the
mess that he created and end up making it worse. he
does not feel those repercussions. not the ones from his
original action or the ones from my actions because of
his action.

he is never sorry for what he does. he is sorry that what
he does hurts me. he apologizes for his actions being
misunderstood, but not for the action itself. he does not
accept that what he does causes problems, only that the
problems are there. never, *i am sorry i said that* but, *i am
sorry you thought that is what i meant.* as if it is my fault,
as if i twisted the situation in my mind and now i am
the one to blame.

"Hypocrite"

you told me
people take.
you told me
only a rare few actually give back.
find them, you said.
don't let people use you and
take you for granted.

funny.

all you did was take,
all you did was use me,
all you did was act like i didn't matter because
maybe i never did.

"Details"

do you miss me?
do you miss what we had?
do you miss
the days we spent cuddled together
like we were afraid to let go?

do you miss
the car rides where we
sang along to the radio and
i had my feet up on the dash?

do you miss
all the laughs we shared,
all the kisses we exchanged,
all the words we spoke,
all the love we gave,
or am i
the only one
missing
you?

"Remainder"

the purple dress. silk. lace. your smile as you saw the
dress sweep across the ground. *a princess*, you said. and
you were my prince.

the hair. braided. pulled back. fancy. danced across my
shoulder. tickled your face. *like a swan*, you said. and
you were my lake.

the nails. painted. red. touched your face. your hands.
on my hips. dancing. music twinkling. *a ballerina*, you
said. and you were my partner.

the heels. silver. sparkles. brought me to your shoulder.
rested my head. *puzzle pieces*, you said. and you were
my other half.

the silky. lacy. purple dress. with the pulled back.
fancy. braided. hair. the red. painted. nails. the sparkly.
silver. shoes. the night that tasted like flowers. like rain.
like every sweet flavor had been placed on our tongues.
but those flavors don't taste so sweet when you are not
my other half anymore. you are not my partner. you are
not my lake. you are not my prince. but you are still all
of that. still a half. still a partner. still a lake. still a
prince. a half with someone else. you have. another
ballerina. another swan. you have. another princess.

"Belonging"

your messy hair as you
first rolled out of bed.
your raspy voice
when you first woke up.
your crooked smile before you
drank your coffee.

it's not mine.
it's not mine anymore.
you are not mine.
your hair isn't mine,
your voice isn't mine,
your smile isn't mine,
your morning self
isn't mine.

it is hers.
it is all hers now.
and somehow,
somehow
i am supposed to be okay
with that.

"Past Tense"

they are delicate words,
was
is
will.

what *was*
is not what *is*
nor what *will* be.

a few letters can completely change the meaning.
because you *were* mine
and *aren't* anymore
nor *will* you ever be again.

"Bent"

every morning,
you made coffee.
added sugar because you liked life
sweet.
you folded pages in books
but hated the damage it left behind.
you liked driving with
windows down
music blaring
because it made you feel closer to the world.
you smoked cigarettes because
you liked taking risks.

and what am i supposed to do now
when i know everything about you,
all the small details i once loved,
and you are gone
and left me as damaged
as the pages in the books
you used to read.

"Devotion"

don't you get it?
you are all i ever wanted.
so don't tell me that i never loved you
because that is all i ever did.

"Betrayal"

why did you give me so much
if you knew i would fall in love with
what you left behind?

why did you give me so much
if you knew i would believe in
every word,
every look,
every smile?

why would you give me so much
if you knew
in the end
you would leave?

"Silent Truth"

you won't know.
you won't know these words are about you.
they aren't all, of course.
but ~~some of them~~
~~a lot of them~~
most of them.

maybe you will know.
maybe you always knew
what you meant to me.
or probably not.
which is why you won't know
that as you read this
it is you.
in all of the poems i shared it was you.

and part of me is afraid if you know,
but part of me?
part of me hopes you do know
and that reading this
breaks your heart.

"Time Travel"

you used to tell me
you hated the past because
life is better in the present,
but i disagree.

how am i supposed to love the present
more than the past
when you were here
and no longer are?

"Heart of Mine"

my heart.
i do not thank it enough for all it does.
all the pain it takes, all the heartbreaks it suffers,
all that it does for me in spite of it.

my heart.
i do not appreciate that it beats inside my chest
regardless of its scars, regardless of its bruises,
regardless of the wounds that
i have caused.

my heart.
it is heavy with every word i have not spoken and
every person i have ever loved.
(those same people who never loved me.)

my heart.
it carries the pain and does not
complain or whine or cry out.
it just keeps beating.

my heart.
it grows stronger. it does not give up.
it keeps surviving every obstacle.
and maybe *my heart*
is just like me because
so will i.

Depression

Depression steals happiness and fills the emptiness with its version of life, twisted, bent, and dark. It can take years to finally pick up the sword, to be brave enough to climb away from the dark and stop letting it control you. Even then, the memory of the dark seems to follow.

I spent months letting depression poison my mind, but I battled it away by focusing on the people who care about me, all of what truly matters in my life, and the love I have for myself. Sometimes, even years after I already won my fight, I sink into the pit. I have learned it is a battle that never ends, even though I thought I won long ago. It is a battle I am proud to say I am prepared for. I am armed with love for my family and friends and protected by my hobbies and my motivation to see where life will take me. When the dark tries to trick me, I feel the hope in my back pocket, the love in my heart, and the life in my veins, and I know there will never be a time I let depression win. The dark cannot scare me when I carry the light.

Fight the dark. Know that the climb will not be easy, but at the top of that climb, when the dark is behind you and tries to pull your ankles back down, reach for love. Reach for the ever after that is waiting for you.

"Okay"

when i say i am okay,
i do not mean
the kind of okay
you think i do.

i mean the kind of okay
where every day,
every moment,
is a struggle.
i mean the kind of okay
where even just breathing is a difficult task.
i mean the kind of okay
where smiles are plastered on forcefully,
where laughs are faker than the people around me,
where happiness is a distant dream and
sadness is a blanket.

i mean the kind of okay
that isn't okay
at all.

"Actress"

maybe i have been
lying to myself this whole time.
maybe i haven't healed.
maybe i am still that sad, broken person
i was two years ago.
maybe i pretended i was okay because
i wanted it to be true,
because i wanted to be happy.

maybe i lied to others so well that i
didn't even realize i was lying to myself.
maybe i lied to myself so well
that i began to think
i was telling the truth.

"Empire"

you can build
as many lies as you want.
but it only takes
a second
for them to fall apart.

"Sirens"

i do not belong here.
the words are whispered from the walls.
they rise up from the floor,
fall from the ceiling and surround me in
suffocating dust.

i do not belong here.
they fly around my head and make so much noise.
how is it there is only silence?

i do not belong here.
the feeling is overwhelming.
i have to escape these screams,
i have to escape this place that tells me
i do not belong here.

i know, oh god i know.
get me out, release me.
i do not belong,
i do not belong,
why did i ever think i belonged?

i do not belong here.
make it stop.
anything to end these whispers that
sound like screams,

i do not belong here,
i do not belong.

"Frostbite"

my thoughts are swirling around in my head like
they have been caught in a
harsh winter breeze.
they won't stop,
won't let up.
they keep moving,
keep pushing,
keep digging into my skin with cold fingernails
until i cry out in pain.

and even then,
they dig deeper
because the thing about my thoughts is
just like a harsh winter breeze
they will not stop even if it hurts me
because neither the weather nor my thoughts
care about my feelings.

"Prisoner"

i tried to write,
but my thoughts seemed to be trapped
in some sort of prison.
unable to escape,
unable to form words
that would make sense.

because they have been captive to
my poisoned mind for so long,
they learned to accept poison as water,
they learned to swallow it in large doses
and never ask questions
even when it burned their throat,
even when the taste reminded them
of all they were trying to forget.

"Reservation"

my poems speak the words
locked in my heart,
hidden deep in my mind.
my poems speak the words
my mouth
cannot.

"Necessity"

writing.
it is not enough,
it is not enough anymore.
this writing of mine
is not enough.

"What They Teach"

i have been taught how to
cut out my tongue
in order to fit the lies
they try to shove into my
mouth.

i have been taught how to
delete my own ideas,
delete who i am,
in order to
please others and
receive what i deserve and
want.

and maybe
i have also been taught
how to let others decide
who i am allowed to be
and that my happiness
will always come after
everyone else's.

"Detachment"

everyone breaks eventually.
there is only so much one person can take
before they start to lose it.

i am tired of people leaving me.
i am scared to become attached because
they always leave.
i am scared to have love in my life
because when people matter,
when you let them in,
they ruin it every time.
they always have to ruin it.
and if they don't ruin it,
life decides to ruin it for you.

"Weight Lifting"

i do not want to be forgotten.
i do not want to be lost among
hundreds of other faces.
because isn't that all i am?
another person, another face,
one that fades in and out of frames with ease,
one that can be deleted just like that.
new people come in and my memory is gone.

there it goes.
me hanging on and
everyone else letting go.
sometimes it is tiring to be the one carrying it all.

"Bitter Burn"

it is like a bottle of wine, the pouring of me.
in multiple glasses i share myself because
it is far too bitter to give it all to one person,
it is far too bitter to drink the whole bottle
in one sitting.

it is not so much about
dumping myself onto others.
it is more about
pouring bit by bit so
everyone has a sip, so
everyone has a taste
of what it is like to constantly worry
about pouring too much to too many people
and being panicked over how to
take it all back
so only i have to be tortured
by the bitterness.

"Temporary"

i am a pencil
and everyone else is a piece of paper
i leave marks on.
i write and write and write
and pour and pour and pour
so i can leave the impact i want.

but i do not think about the marks being left on me
because i keep writing to make an impression,
to leave a legacy behind.
and my tip becomes duller and duller
until it fades away, until it cannot
write anymore.

and even then
i keep reshaping myself, keep
sharpening myself, so i can continue giving.
and regardless of whether those
pieces of paper care about what i write,
it hurts me because all i do is leave a mark
without realizing the mark being left on me,
without realizing
the permanent damage being done,
without realizing that eventually
i will not be able to keep reshaping myself
because i will have poured too much, because
i will have given all i have to give.

"Hear Me"

would you believe me
if i said
it didn't matter?
would you believe me
if i said
i didn't care?
would you believe me
if i said
it didn't break my heart?

or would you believe the truth?
which is that
it matters a lot.
which is that
i care way more than i should.
which is that
my heart is absolutely shattered.
which is that
i am absolutely ruined.

"Behind Closed Doors"

you call her a bitch. you are yelling without even knowing what is coming out of your mouth. you walk away, too annoyed to apologize. she walks away, too. she hurries up to her room, climbs into her bed, and bawls into the pillow. she stares straight ahead of her as she feels like a waste of space, as your words sit with her like a boulder on her chest.

eventually her tears will stop falling and instead a heavy emptiness will fall over her. she will walk around like a zombie until she musters up an apology to you. you only apologize because she did, even though you are not mad. it must be your ego. you feel like you cannot say sorry first. you think it is okay. so you do it again and again and again. you think it is okay because the words are worthless, because you do not mean it, but she does not know that. even if she did, it would not take away the fact that you are hurting her with these invisible punches you cannot take back.

you keep fighting until one day you cross the line. she storms out, and as she is crying in her bed, as she is feeling useless, reviewing the fight in her head over and over until she has it memorized, she thinks about every other fight. she hears your words in her head and they sound too loud, as if blasted through a speaker. and as she is staring straight ahead of her like she always does, she wonders why she is even fighting when her heart is giving up. she wonders what is left to fight for.

so think about that the next time you want to call her a bitch. because you might be slowly pushing her toward the edge, until you give her the final shove.

"Locked Box"

she has learned to hide secrets
the same way she has learned to hide
the bruises he gives her.
we all learn by repetition.
she learned to keep secrets in a box without a key,
learned to stuff parts of herself into that box.
she built another part of herself
separate from the girl she actually is.

which would explain why
she gave herself to boys she did not love.
which would explain why
she pushed away the love she deserved
just because she could.

because we learn by repetition.
she taught herself how to be someone else.
she taught herself how to give away her choices.
she taught herself how to say,
this is not my life anymore.

"Switch"

she had her moments. she had her moments where
you would talk, and she would smile her bright smile
that lit up the entire room, such a magnificent smile
that reached her eyes, and you could see that they
were filled with such happiness and joy. they would
twinkle like stars, each shining brighter than the
moon.

but she also had her moments where she was so sad
she wanted to put the knife to her neck instead of her
wrists. where her eyes were filled with such despair,
you could not even look into them. they were eyes
grayer than ash.

and that's the problem with sadness: it begins to feel
like home.

"Invisibility"

when an object breaks,
it is really easy for it to break again.
a cracked vase
will shatter more easily than
one that is perfectly fine.

that is why
you have to be careful with people:
you cannot always see
their cracks.

"Cliff"

you remember what it feels like to be that sad.
you remember feeling
useless, worthless, like you weren't
important at all.
you felt like nobody needed you and
you would never be enough.
it took you forever to heal from it.
you clawed and climbed and fought like hell
to escape from the hole you were plunged into.

sometimes,
your foot slips from the top and you
fall a little ways down.
you start remembering what
those feelings were like.
you think about letting go completely and falling
all the way back down
and you would have to start over
from the very beginning.

"At War with Myself"

i am torn between feeling sorry for myself,
like i am a good person who deserves better,
and feeding into their words.
maybe when people say i am mean or that i
do not deserve good,
they are right.
maybe i really am horrible.

then i remember all those
uplifting poems, how they say to
always stand up for yourself and have self-love.
i am stuck in the middle, battling away
the heartbreaking words echoing in my head.
i am trying desperately
not to let them hurt me.

but how do i push away words that
stick to my skin like they have been glued there,
how do i not care about
words i remember months later like they have been
tattooed into my mind,
how do i not listen to words that remind me of
how much i hate myself?

"Endless Battle"

the past. it is a chain on my wrists. i try to fight it the same way the waves battle the moon, but i was stupid to believe i could break free of its gravity. i was stupid to believe i could release the shackles binding my wrists.

i am stuck dragging it around, mercilessly battling its memories. the chains dig into my delicate skin and chafe it away, turning it red raw. my wrists are bleeding as the salt stings my wounds.

and as i hit the shore, ready to reach for the future, i am pulled back so the salt bites me again. i am forever trying to reach something i cannot have. because tomorrow is always out of grasp. and today is inescapable. and yesterday forever follows me and haunts me because i can never touch it or change it even though it is right there. like the moon casts a shadow on the sand. the same sand i am constantly chasing.

the past. touches everything. the past. never lets us go.

"Lungs"

i emerge from the waves and
cough on air.
because i spent
so long drowning,
i forgot how to breathe.

<u>Moving On</u>

Moving on from love is never easy. Sometimes we want to let go but can't. Sometimes we do not want to let go but have to. Whether someone rushes away suddenly or slowly leaves us behind, whether we pick up and run or walk while looking back, if it is in the past, if it hurts us, we have to move on. If it heals us, we can carry it without letting it hurt, without gripping onto it so tightly that we have burn marks on our hands.

I am constantly moving on from people I love, moments I cherish, and places I cannot go back to. My heart hates spitting out the word goodbye and letting go of love. The hardest part is not leaving behind what hurts me; it is leaving behind what makes me smile. I cannot keep everything I want to keep, but I know I abandon the gloom so I can grow as a person. I know I abandon the good so I can carry it in my back pocket. Every person, in their own way, stays in my heart.

Let go of what hurts you. Even if life forces you to release what you want to keep, know that people, moments, and places are left behind to make room for what comes next.

"These Walls"

you can break me down,
beat me to tiny little pieces.
you can destroy who i am and
make me someone i'm not.

but you can't
hurt me anymore.
because i built these walls
to keep out the pain.
i built these walls
to save my heart.
i built these walls
to keep away
people like
you.

"Finish Line"

i am over you.
so don't come back.
because i am done.
i am done with you and
i am done with hanging onto you.

"Becoming What I Thought You Wouldn't"

you used to ask me why i hated boys.
you would put on your flirtatious smile and
rest your chin on your hand while i answered,
listing off each item that did not include you.

you never fit the description for what i
hated about boys.
but now, while i am living my life
and you are living yours separately,
i am wondering where i went wrong.
i am wondering why you don't text me anymore.
i am wondering why you never
explained your change of heart.

if you asked me the same question now,
i would tell you that
what you are currently doing to me,
leaving me wondering what i did wrong because
you left with no explanation,
is exactly why i hate boys.
it is exactly why i hate you.

"Puppetry"

i am not a toy.
you cannot pick me up and play with me
and decide later that
you don't want me anymore.

"Never After"

they say every story has an ending, but
endings give you closure
and i never got that from you.
- *our story finished, but*
  there was never an ending.

"Relapse"

i tell everyone my story with you,
the one where i loved someone
who did not love me back.
i smile and roll my eyes at how
stupid all of it was.

for the most part i believe it.
i believe that i am over it, over you.
i believe that i have moved on from
that part of my life.

but there are moments when i am
thinking back to you and your smile
and your hypnotizing voice and i am
daydreaming about what could
have happened with you
and i find myself smiling at the memories
i wish we had created and i wonder if
i have really moved on at all.

"Unfulfilled"

i promised myself.
i promised myself i would stop
talking about you so much,
thinking about you so much,
writing about you so much.

i promised myself.
that i would not keep hanging onto you,
that i would not keep loving you.
that i would move on and be happy.

i promised myself.
promised that my heart would not stay broken,
that it would not keep beating for you,
that it would find someone new to love.

i promised myself.
but maybe,
just like you,
i am only good at breaking promises.

"Capabilities"

my feelings are there.
i don't want them because sometimes it feels like
they ruin me,
but i will reluctantly let them in.

i will let myself go on the
rollercoaster of liking someone.
i will let myself enjoy all the times that
he laughs and the way he looks at me.
i will hate it and guilt over it all the while, and
i will hate it more than accept it,
but i will enjoy it.
and absolutely hate myself for it at the same time.

i am who i am.
i am human.
i mess up.
but i can forgive.

"The One who Never Cared (and never will)"

darling lover that never loved me anyway,

i never stopped loving you.
i never stopped thinking about
the words you said that
made me fall for you.
sometimes i wonder if it
could have happened
only if you had truly loved me,
truly cared,
but you never did.

i find myself
clearly remembering how you looked
when you laughed,
but i know as much as
i wish you were kind
you aren't,
and i know i need to
move on from you
but i can't.

"Bad Habits"

letting go of someone you love is like
having dry lips.
you know if you lick them
they will be worse,
but you cannot seem to stop yourself.
you just keep going back to
an obsession that
hurts you.

"Toxin"

you still love him after
what he did to you.
after he made you suffer for
all that time, let you
slowly melt away.
you convince yourself
what you had with him was real,
but maybe for a second consider that
it wasn't love at all:
it was poison.

"Trying"

i want to let you go, but
i'm not sure that
i know how.

"100 Words For You"

i am beginning to let you go, but
i am far from moving on.
i still love you with everything i have.
(it is the only way i know how to love.)

but i am accepting you are gone.
it hurts but not as much.
i miss you but not as painfully.
it is slowly healing.
my love is not dying, but the
pain of the memories no longer feels like
a knife in my side.

i will let you go, but i could never move on.
because loving you with everything
left every piece of me
in your hands.

"Until We Meet"

this is my goodbye to you,
to my future lover.
i cannot hang onto you anymore.
it is hurting me too much
to want someone
i will not have for years,
so i am letting you go
until there is someone
i can actually hang onto.

"Deserted"

you are gone.
gone like the sun when the night takes over,
gone like the tide when it pulls back.
gone like erased pencil marks,
gone like the taste of brownies after
milk has washed it away.

gone like warm air at the beginning of winter,
like swimsuits when jackets replace them.
gone like the smell of a new book's pages.
gone like memories
when too much time has passed.
gone like the words flowing from my pen.
because when you are gone,
i have no more reason to write.

"Prohibited"

the words
we cannot do this anymore
are on the tip of my tongue.
right there,
so close.

so close, i can taste them in my mouth.
so close, i can feel them dance across my skin.
so close, i can feel them resonate in my bones.
so close, i almost say them.
but i don't.

i cannot bring myself to say them because
that would mean letting you go,
that would mean giving up, and
i do not give up on the things i love.

instead,
the words wrap around my entire body
trying to choke me,
strangle me,
so maybe the words will
fall out anyway.

"Migration"

i was looking at you
and in that second,
i wondered where all my feelings had gone.
they seemed to fly away.
they seemed to realize they weren't where
they were supposed to be.

for that second,
they had a brain.
they knew it was wrong to hold onto you.
because like birds,
feelings fly home.
they always find a way home.
and even if only for a second,
they knew my home was not with you.

"Tug-of-War"

eventually you learn.
you learn that some people are
too painful to hang onto
so you let them go.
even if you fought like hell to keep them.
because you should never try to
hold onto someone
who does not fight to keep you.

"For Me"

i am holding onto what you did,
remembering each and every time you hurt me.
i am killing myself slowly by
bringing you up in my daily thoughts.

so i forgive you.
not for you, but for me.
i forgive all of your words, and
i forgive all of your actions.
i am not forgiving you because you are
sorry or because what you did was okay,
but because
i need to forgive you so i can move on.

"Reflection"

saying goodbye to you is one of the
biggest challenges i have ever faced.
but if it was not hard,
it would mean it did not matter.

"Appreciation"

i had no idea
where this was going to take me.
i could not have known that it would
lead to me making unforgettable memories
and meeting someone
who has touched my life and
helped shape who i am.

but maybe fate knew how it would end.
maybe fate knew that
i would have an amazing experience.
like fate knew i would create moments
that would stay in my heart
long after they had left my life.
like fate knew that
even when it was over,
i would be happy i had it while it lasted.

"Loving You"

this is it.
this is my goodbye.
my goodbye to what happened with you,
my goodbye to the way i loved you.

i am out of words.
i do not even know what to say anymore
because i have said it all.
from the heartbreak to the sadness
to the unrequited love.
i have written about the times i
cried myself to sleep about what you said
or what you didn't say.
i have written about
what i learned from loving you and
how i overcame it.

so i am saying goodbye to you.
because you do not love me
and it is not worth my loving you.

"Our Story"

words can no longer describe you.
the way you made me feel or
the memories we created.
words, for once, are failing me.

so maybe it is a sign.
a sign that i should no longer write
words in this book.
a sign that the chapters are complete,
the sentences perfected.
i will close it,
let it sit on the bookshelf and gather dust.

maybe i will pick it up occasionally.
flip through the pages.
remember what we had.
remember what we shared.
remember that even though we are
not writing more in the book of our love,
i will smile because once
once upon a time
what we had was beautiful.

A Thank You

to my parents for supporting me. thank you for letting me be myself and follow even the craziest of dreams. both of you have given me more than i could ever give back, and i hope one day i will find the words to properly thank you for it.

to my sisters for providing unwavering love and constant encouragement. both of you inspire me to reach for the stars, and i want you to know that i only try in hopes that i will be able to bring some back for you.

to my entire family for reminding me how lucky i am to have people who believed i could do it before we even knew what *it* was going to be.

to my friends for understanding me. for listening. for making me laugh. for the memories i will never forget. for being my strength when i wasn't sure i had the ability to stand.

to the ones in this book for allowing it to be written. each of you gave me memories worth writing about, and whether you are in one poem or most of these poems, you all matter. this book was my way to give you a gift more permanent than what we shared, my way to say thank you. even if you will never know you are being thanked.

to you, the reader, for giving the time to hold my heart. i hope you leave these pages with what you came here to find. i hope you know how grateful i am to have shared my journey with you. it means more than you could ever know.

Brynne Aidlin-Perlman is a fifteen-year old from Massachusetts who breathes words and pours her heart into her writing. In addition to poetry, she spends time singing and acting. She has a passion for the stage, and in 2018, she acted in a production for the annual METG Drama Festival, a statewide competition with over 100 participating schools where her high school ranked in the top three. Brynne also performs her poetry, allowing her to combine two of her favorite pastimes. She is very grateful to be able to grow in different creative ways and hopes to keep the arts woven into her life.

For more of Brynne's poetry, access her social media page:

Instagram: @L0ving.you